A Shopper's Guide to Dating!
For Men and Women

Jacqui Hill Goudeau

Copyright © 2016 Jacquelyn Hill Goudeau

All rights reserved. No part of this publication may be reproduced, stored in a retrieval system, or transmitted in any form by means electronic, mechanical, photocopying, recording or otherwise, except the inclusion of brief quotations in a review, without prior permission in writing from the publisher.

Cover Design Updated 2026

ISBN-13: 978-0-9896233-3-9

DEDICATION

To the God I love, Who is Love.

ACKNOWLEDGMENTS
Special thanks to
Bishop Shelton Bady, Brian R. Johnson, John C.E. Hudson,
Tony W. Goudeau, and Ernestine Rhodes

Thank You!
To everyone who took part in our "Shopping Survey" –
Your insight was priceless.

Taylor Goudeau, Sharon Hill Morris, James Jordan, Be Jota, Sheyenne Morris, DeLisa Perry, Natashia Wright, Dacora Walker, Ron Stallings, Chris Larry, Brandon Larry, Savanna Sam, Vanessa Quillen, Brian Thomas, Alan Harris, Sobreta Harris, Nana Kyei Amponsah, Nikki Shaw, Debra Aboagye, Kathy P, Michae'la Franklin, Margo Franklin, Tamekia Franklin, Lorna Fox, BJC, Shonice Reed, E. Broussard, Dannie Kelly, Natalie Zuniga, Cyd Taylor, Mosadi Porter, Jackie Williams, Donnetta Johnson, as well as many others (mostly men) who chose to be anonymous!

The SHOPPING CART

- Confessions of a Non-Shopper! — Pg. 1
- Shopping and Dating — Pg. 5
- The Shopping List: Spirit, Soul, Body — Pg. 19
- The Fitting Room — Pg. 37
- The Alterations Shop — Pg. 47
- Unrealistic Expectations: Knock Offs — Pg. 57
- The Shopper's Guide for Women — Pg. 67
- The Shopper's Guide for Men — Pg. 71
- On The Market! — Pg. 79
- Shopaholics vs. Dateaholics — Pg. 87
- Layaway! — Pg. 91
- Final Thoughts — Pg. 93
- About the Author — Pg. 97

CONFESSIONS OF A NON-SHOPPER

People always ask me, "What woman doesn't like shopping?" There was a time if you asked me, I would simply tell you, "I don't like shopping." But over the past few years, I have grown a bit more fond of it. Not liking to shop has traditionally been the cry of men, but I have met men who shop more than I do and enjoy it. I enjoyed it at one time…that is before I started working in retail.

That was the beginning of my downward spiral. Too many holidays and weekends spent behind a counter or register with sometimes ungrateful customers who were "always right."

I remember when stores weren't open on holidays or Sundays in Texas, but I also remember when it began to change. I spent many evenings picking clothing off the ground or folding sweaters over and over again. We worked so many hours especially with special sales and markdowns that had to be done before the crowds bombarded the doors. That could have been the last straw for me, but there were worse times in retail. Those times were spent in the fitting room. This is where you really learned a lot about people. No one wanted to work in the fitting room! That was the place where clothes were flung on a rail or left in a pile with pants legs turned inside out or sleeves twisted in knots. You might even find the occasional Pamper left in a room by a mother who didn't take time to ask for a trash can. Yep, I probably lost my urge to splurge in the fitting rooms of life. Though that was years ago, it still affects me today. I often cringe at the thought of shopping. I don't like fitting rooms, and I don't like standing in long lines with only two registers open. I don't enjoy rummaging through clothes placed in the wrong sizes and piles of sale items thrown on a table for us to fight over. The weird contrast is that I love looking for things for my house, or stopping by the home improvement stores, even window shopping, but somehow I lost interest in shopping for ME.

A few years ago, I made a commitment to myself to get over my shopping-phobia, so I started by scheduling myself to shop at least once a month. I didn't have to purchase something every time, but I had to go and see what was out there, what I liked that was new, and exciting. By doing this, I started to learn to shop in a way that suits me. No malls or Black Friday sales, no going through piles of clothes thrown together in a clearance area. Specialty shops were the way to go. I have also discovered the joy and convenience of online shopping, and of course, I still like window shopping. I prefer shopping early in the day, when most people are at work and their kids are in school, a time when the workers are still fresh in their day and likely to be more courteous.

It used to be when I shopped, there was something in particular I was looking for. If it was black shoes, you wouldn't find me in another area. I headed right to the shoe section with my radar on to find and conqueror the black shoe. Now I have learned to open my eyes to see what I might like that I was <u>not</u> looking for, or wouldn't have considered before. As a result, I have found many treasures that I truly enjoy simply because I decided to **open my mind to new possibilities**.

In this book, we will examine our shopping habits and see how they match up with our dating habits. You will be surprised by how similar they are. By examining simple human patterns, you may find out something about yourself that will help you shop your life differently. Even if your habits are good ones for who you are, this book will at least shed some light on who you are, and why you shop or date the way you do. So, are you ready? If so, open your mind, put on your shopping shoes, and expect to have fun as we begin our shopping spree.

SHOPPING AND DATING

There is nothing wrong with knowing what you want.

It took me quite a while to write this book. When I first came up with the idea, I was married and thought singles really wouldn't be interested in what a married woman had to say about the subject of dating. After all, I had been out of the game for quite a while. Since then, my 20-year marriage dissolved, and I am once again unmarried. With a few single years under my belt, this seems like the perfect time to tackle this topic.

I have counseled and talked to many single people over the years, men and women alike. Some have asked these simple questions:

"What is wrong with me that I can't find a husband?" "How can she get a man and I can't?" The men say, *"I am a good man.*

Women don't want a good man anymore." or *"Women are too picky. No one is going to fit the bill they give you."*

When you hear these questions and comments, it might sound like they are throwing off on someone else, but in those sessions, it was more a cry of their heart concerning what might be wrong with them or how could they become more attractive to the right person and not lose themselves in the process. One of the purposes of this book is to help us see what we are looking for and what patterns we display that could be hindering us from finding it. Sometimes we are unaware of how we appear to others, and they have no clue how they appear to us. Dressing up and smelling good is fine, but when you are looking for a forever relationship, you should consider a holistic set of priorities. By examining simple shopping habits, we can learn quite a bit about ourselves and what we are doing or not doing that affects who we attract or dispel. Let's examine some simple yet general shopping and dating habits. As we continue, think about your own practices. Since we are so unique in our makeup, you may basically guide yourself in what to adjust in your world of shopping vs. dating.

SHOPPING:

My earliest memory of shopping was in my mother's catalogs. Popular department stores like Sears and JC Penney's mailed catalogs to customers' homes. There was no such thing as online shopping, so this was the closest thing to it. My sisters and I would sit and look through every page of each catalog and say, *"That is mine..." "That is yours..." "That's mine..."* (of course, claiming the best looking items for ourselves.) We played this game with clothing, furniture, household items, and even the men! *"That's your husband..." "That's mine..."* At such an early age, we were already learning to "shop" or basically mold our minds to determine our likes and dislikes. No one was really dating- that wouldn't come for years, but we were learning to "shop." Newspapers back in that day were simple black and white publications, but the catalogs were colorful and full of clothes that were stylish, and everyone looked happy and rich! Our minds were unwittingly moving away from simple, informative, or meaningful things and drawn to the flashy, stylish, and popular. We would turn page after page looking at the skillfully placed models in their perfectly planned attire. Of course, we were kids, we had no money, no jobs… we weren't buying anything. But we had the ability to dream *way* beyond our means! One of the joys of shopping is dreaming, dreaming and being able to search for and find the thing that works for you. Standing in front of the mirror imagining where you would wear it, how it would fit in your wardrobe, and don't forget the attention it would draw! The perfect suit and tie, the perfect dress, the perfect pair of shoes, or the perfect accessories, we like the thrill of finding something unexpected that we think works for us.

Now, depending on who you are and how you are wired, the cost may not matter to you. Some shoppers only look for deals. Part of their shopping joy is in not having to pay too much, maybe even being able to set their own price. Other shoppers crave the quality and will pay whatever it takes to get it. Neither one is wrong, just different. But if you have a habit of only looking for a deal, or if you spend thinking that cost alone means quality, that does not work in relationships. You may find that sometimes the price ends up being more than you bargained for or the basic quality for a "deal" is lacking.

SHOPPING ON PURPOSE

If you are like me, you don't shop just to shop. I typically have a goal in mind and then I shop. Since many of us have similar habits, some of us may shop based on whatever our immediate need/want is. Others may be avid window shoppers, shopaholics, bargain shoppers, professional shoppers, or a non-shoppers with a need to fill. Whatever your style or reason, it is still good to know what you want. Knowing what you genuinely want or need is important.

Growing up, we lived a short time in a children's home in El Paso, Texas. Every Sunday evening my mom would drop us off for the week and we would stay at 'The Home', go to school from there, and return home with my mom on Fridays. Since the only personal clothing we had was what we wore there, we depended on them for everything else. The Home had closets full of donated clothes that we wore every day for school and play. We sported our own clothes on Fridays when we were scheduled to return home with our parents for the weekend. During the week, it took us so long to find what we wanted to wear for school. It was almost like shopping when we picked out our clothes. Some of us would take our time because we knew what we wanted, but there was a great possibility that it was not there, or that someone else already had it. What we wore to school every day was an extension of us, our personality, and determined how we felt about ourselves the next day, or how we thought other students felt about us. After searching through a closet full of hand me downs, you had to decide and just get something to wear to school. There were no other options.

Life is not that rigid. Relationships should never be diminished to just finding something before the time runs out. Sometimes you just have to be honest about whether or not the places you are looking can provide what you genuinely want. Instead of settling for what looks like your only option, consider a change in where and how you shop.

PAYING THE PRICE!

Some shoppers will pay whatever it costs to get what they want. In their mind, knowing it's what they want, justifies the price. For others, if we are not careful, we can easily be distracted by sales or promotions and forget what we originally set out to get. There's nothing wrong with knowing what you want. If you know you can afford something or if you are willing to pay the price and it won't break your budget, then buy it! But if you realize the price is more than you feel comfortable with or more than you planned to pay, you may need time. It is better to know what you want and adjust the shopping list if you realize what you want is not what you need. Too often, buying on a whim can result in bringing home items you realize looked better on the dummy.

By now you have probably grasped the essence of this book, so without me trying to describe your personal shopping style, let's go into the dating aspect.

DATING:

Growing up, I was not a big dater. (It already sounds like my shopping.) I can recall on one hand the guys early on who were interested in me, at least the ones who admitted it. During my early 20s, I could tell you what I wanted in a husband and it didn't seem as if anyone fit that bill. Since I had an idea of what I wanted, I would instantly notice whoever <u>didn't</u> have those qualities more than I would notice anyone who did, and I would stay away. I didn't consider whether I was expecting too much or if they had better qualities than the ones on my little list. Being so narrow minded didn't help me get any more dates. After a while, men felt that I was unapproachable or uninterested, so they didn't come around anymore. Since I was single and living alone, this approach kept me out of a lot trouble, but it also kept a few good men away.

Sometimes when we are dating, we may not consider the big picture. We just see the appeal of the catalog. Remember the black and white newspaper? It held the least appeal when shopping, the catalog was the best way to dream. Today our newspapers have learned how to add color, fashion, style, and a little appeal, but my training in shopping was in catalogs. It took me a while to realize that men who were simple, with a good head on their shoulders, not flashy but nice, were actually a good catch! Not every man is a CEO of a company with presidential aspirations, and the few who are may **actually be** *looking for someone similar.*

In my childlike ways, I had learned to shop and dream beyond my means. I learned how to dream about a relationship that I couldn't afford, a relationship that I didn't have what it took to get, much less keep.

Singles who are looking for the sex appeal in a man or woman often forget about other qualities that will benefit them in the long run. There is nothing wrong with wanting the "look," but that is the one thing that is guaranteed to change. Being reluctant to connect with a "newspaper person" can result in some of us missing out on a really great connection. We have to know more about ourselves and what we genuinely want and need in this life if we want to date effectively.

DATING ON PURPOSE

Dating is one of those things some people just like to do. Some love to date for fear of being alone or viewed as not being desirable. If you, man or woman, have no clue as to what your purpose is, you should probably **not** be dating. Don't get me wrong. There is nothing wrong with hanging out with someone and enjoying an evening, nothing wrong with meeting people and having fun. But if your plan for dating is the bigger picture, be honest with yourself. If you think of dating as an exclusive relationship that you hope will one day turn permanent, then you have to take it more seriously. Dating is a very personal thing, but it is time consuming and can be mentally and emotionally draining. Gone should be the days of dating just because you are lonely. That is what friends, family, children, and your PURPOSE are for. Your purpose will fill time like no one else can. My pastor said years ago:

"Loneliness is not the absence of affection,

but the absence of direction."

When you know what you are born to do, when you know your purpose in life, you can find things to occupy any down time. You don't need someone to fill your life to make you feel whole. Your purpose does that. But of course, we are relational people, and knowing what your purpose is, how you are wired and what makes you happy can only add to the dating process. So if you are one of those who really wants to date to marry, you can't afford to date for the joy of 'just' dating. You should know what you want and what you require. This also includes knowing what PRICE you are willing to pay to ensure that whoever you hook up with is happy, too.

I recently spent time with an old friend, and we had a list for each day we hung out. On our list were things like:

What is his purpose? What is mine? How do they connect? Do they need to connect? Does he have to do what I do? What are our long-term goals? What are our short-term goals? If you could change anything in your past, what would it be? What makes you happy? What do you dislike? Why did any previous relationships fade? What did you learn about yourself?

When it came to our purposes being the same, I found the answer was no. My purpose is mine, his is his. It is great if they complement each other, but we don't both have to be politicians, accountants, teachers, or doctors to have a good connection. It is just understanding what each of us are born to do, and respecting that. It is knowing what it takes for each of us to be successful, and being willing to do our part to support that.

We talked about what we liked and didn't like, what we planned for our kids, and where we were going in life. We spoke of our life goals and whether or not they sounded similar. At that point, if it didn't match, it was OK. We were just talking. No wrong answers, no need to amaze… answers given truthfully were the RIGHT answers. Trying to impress someone can result in wrong information and bad connections. Attempting to be what someone wants opposite of who you are, is a problem. (Read chapter 6: Unrealistic Expectations: Knock Offs)

SHOPPING HUNGRY

We have heard for the longest that it is best not to go shopping hungry because you are likely to overspend. The same applies to dating. Desperation can show up if you are too needy. The worst thing to do is to go shopping RIGHT when you want a need met. You have less time and more pressure to find what you want. Many times we will know that someone is not what we want or need and just to date… there we go. You are less likely to hold to personal standards and less likely to follow your heart- or God's. Shopping or dating in desperation, is a serious no, no. That mindset can lead to **shoplifting.** (acting, praying, and falsely believing someone is for you without their buy in.)

We see this often when someone 'tells' you that God has revealed that you are their spouse. I have known women that have purchased wedding dresses for a man who does not even know she exists, and men who have purchased rings for a woman that keeps telling him she is uninterested. Just a note for those who find themselves in this predicament. Know that God does NOT override our will. There are very few people in the bible that God chose their spouse for them. Some specifically asked God to guide them to the right person, other times God was making a point. The majority of us are going to be responsible for whoever we decide to marry. We have been given opportunity to ask for God's help, and the help of others. So if anyone you approach sends the message that they are not interested, move on. There really are a lot of options that can work for you.

THINK ABOUT IT

Take some time to think about your shopping style and your dating style. Only you really know what goes through your mind when you do either one. Dating with so many expectations and a list so long that literally no one can meet it will not help you make a good connection. Spending most of your time running from place to place looking for someone is tiring, draining, and discouraging.

Our ultimate goal should be understood before we even consider dating - so start with the end in mind. If you have no desire to marry or settle down, admit it! At least you can try to avoid the "fatal attractions" that won't let you go later. Being able to communicate what you want and need before getting involved will help your heart and theirs. Thinking we are the only one with a standard sets us up for a fail. Remember, someone is looking at you just as you are looking at them.

THE SHOPPING LIST

I am, by nature, a list maker. People have told me that I have issues, and I know I do. You can tell me almost anything, and if I don't write it down, I might forget it. Since I know this about myself, I make lists for just about everything. Grocery list, to-do list. I make a list from my voicemail at work and cross each name off as I return the call. Even on my days off, I have a list of things I want to accomplish before days end. If I don't get to it, it remains on the list for the next time. So it was not really strange that years ago in my early 20s, I wrote a list of what I wanted in a spouse. Typical of me, I separated my list into three different categories.

1. Spirit
2. Soul
3. Body

Over the years, I have encouraged many unmarried people to do the same. It is not that the list is a letter to God that He is obligated to fill. There is nothing magical about making a list. But one thing the list does is make you think. It prompts you to ask questions like:

- What do I really want?
- What am I not willing to settle for?
- What do I have on this list that might really be unnecessary?
- What am I willing to adjust in me?
- What on my list may be there out of pride?

The list is subject to you and what God is doing in you. Sometimes it has to be adjusted based on changes He is making in you and how you think. Some of those changes happen because of age, maturity, and wisdom. So when you write your list, understand that you may have to adjust it later. To begin your list, I recommend you start with: Spirit.

The Spirit

Light-Life-Love

The most spiritual thing you can do as an individual is to connect with the One who made you, and connect with why you were made.

When making your list, you should ask yourself:

- What spiritual attributes do I want from someone I would consider being in a committed relationship with?
- What level of relationship do they need to have with God?
- What moral standards are important to me? To God?
- Is there an attribute they need that God requires?

This area of SPIRIT can often be difficult to determine. One reason is because we find ourselves in a place of feeling like we are judging whether we think someone is spiritual enough for us… especially if we don't really deem ourselves that spiritual to begin with. If we are not very spiritual people, we can assume this is not an area necessary to list. But trust me, this area can make or break a lot in relationships.

For those who are a bit more spiritual, they can end up thinking more highly of themselves and think what they need is a person who sits on the right hand of God Himself.

We have basically been taught as believers that being unequally yoked is wrong. We read that in scripture, but we don't think about what it look like to be <u>equally</u> yoked.

Typically oxen would be yoked up with another one that is similar so that their movements would make a straight line. If there were too many core differences, it would affect the overall goal. They complemented each other as they worked because they worked together. If you have two strong-willed cattle pulling in opposite directions, they can tear up the land. That is considered unequally yoked, not the fact that the two have some differences. Being unequally yoked with unbelievers is seen in the same way - two headstrong people who view life or goals in opposite ways. The same applies to business partners or any other person you would connect with on purpose. If they are as strong as you are with opposite goals, you will get nowhere. Most of us don't argue the issues of having a basic belief system that is the same. From your SPIRIT comes all the thoughts you have about right and wrong, about the meaning of life, and who or how we love. This area along with our SOUL will determine how we raise our children. It is important enough to take time to see that you fit in this area. If the core similarities can't be found, keep shopping. The easiest and quickest way to answer some of these concerns is to ask yourself, "Is this person a growing Christian?" They may not be all grown up, but neither are we! We will always have to leave room for growth in the other person and in ourselves as well.

Purpose Connection

They used to say behind every great or successful man, is a great or successful woman. It often sounded like that was her only purpose. If we really think about it, the best relationships are forged when both parties have discovered their own purpose and realize what they do fits with the other person. When we have values and standards that govern our spiritual life, it allows a connection from the deepest part of us. It allows us to completely be ourselves with the person we want to spend life with. The most spiritual thing you can do as an individual is to connect with the One who made you and connect with why you were made. If you find someone who has done this, there is less to wonder about in this area and more to look forward to together.

So make your shopping list! Think about yourself, your purpose, and what you need on your list. What things will help you be who you are supposed to be? What Spiritual connection do they need?

The Soul

Mind-Will-Emotions

We sometimes forget that someone's relationship with God will ensure they make it to heaven, but the soul area may determine whether as a couple, you have heaven or hell on earth!

This is the area that is a lot of fun, but it is also the area where many couples can fail. Just because someone is a good person does not mean they are the right fit for you. In an attempt to ensure that we have someone who loves God, is connected to their purpose, and living a good life with personal standards, we sometimes forget that we are the one who will be living with them!

Years ago I said I wanted someone who would love God more than they loved me. Back then it sounded really noble and Christ like, but I realize today, should I marry again, he will be marrying ME. Not God. He may be really committed to Him, but I need someone who will love me and be committed to me as well. Someone who will encourage me to follow God's purpose for my life and vice versa.

In many churches, women were often told to be sure any male candidate was a believer, working, and didn't have a lot of women friends. For men, there were not too many guidelines that I can recall except watch out for too many kids, avoid a woman who disrespects you, and guard your wallet. We kind of forgot to encourage people to trust that there was someone out there for THEM.

There is someone you connect with who works for you and you for them. Stop acting as if God is going to pick your spouse. He will guide you but this selection is really yours. You have to live with them! So when you fill out your shopping list, remember… this is for you. If we were talking about clothing, you would consider that YOU have to wear those shoes, that dress, dress shirt, or that suit. If it is too tight, or is irritating at the neckline, though others may think it looks good, you have to live with whatever you take home. If it is not comfortable for you, you won't wear or display it much at all. It becomes a look and feel you are not happy with and you can't wait to get home and get out of. (relationships too)

In the Soul area, you may want someone you can talk and laugh with. Anyone too serious might mess you up, or you them. If you are a serious type, someone too silly may not work for you. You may want someone who enjoys and deals well with children, working in the yard and actually enjoys cleaning the house! Someone who is dull, messy, and does not talk at all might make you wonder or wander. The same if you are a laid back person who may not clean every minute of the day. You have to know yourself well enough to ensure you are not going to drive each other crazy.

Bottom line, you have to know what price you are willing to pay for what you want. We often hear that opposites attract, and they do, but it is powerful only if both parties realize the gift in each other and embrace it. If one loves doing finances and the other is not good at it, you decide by how you act, whether or not the difference is a blessing or a curse. The same with similarities. No matter how similar you are, there are differences in the midst! Opposites work when we know how to yield and allow for the other's strength, much like fingers mingling to make one fist. We can choose to learn and experience the benefits of each other.

We all have the ability to drive folks crazy. This is often seen in the things we like that others don't, the things we embrace that others don't, the ways we are that others aren't. The differences can drive us! We all want to be in a relationship where we are celebrated, not just tolerated. Knowing yourself is key in the soul area, because it deals with your mind, will, and emotions. Emotions can take over a relationship if you are not careful. A stubborn will can dictate what you are going to do or not do. Nothing can make you change outside a traumatic or relational collision in your life. You have to know yourself before you fill out your shopping list. If I am allergic to peanuts, why would my list contain peanut butter? The list helps you walk briskly through the store, purposefully. What this means in relationships and dating is this:

Be honest with yourself. Don't thread people along just for a date or a good night out. If you already know they do not meet some main criteria on your list, why make them think there is a chance? Knowing how to be kind when you release someone and treat people with respect is one of the attributes we forget people see in us every day. We have to know if something is not going to work, and be honest… Now if NO ONE can meet your criteria, you may need to talk to God and adjust your list.

SOUL TIES: Too much time spent?

One thing I often tell people, "You have to be aware of who you hang with, because you can fall in love with almost anyone". Why would I say that? Because time, attention, and familiarity mean something. We often call this a "soul tie." Soul ties are not just formed from sexual relationships you engage in, though that is the primary way we've heard of them. Your mind can connect with someone after a lot of time spent in long conversations on the phone, talking about life or hurts, or just hanging together can cause your emotions to connect. Someone who makes you feel important can hide the fact they have attributes you really can't stand.

Love is not really blind. We just allow our minds to be clouded to the things we have already seen. Don't waste your time. Guard your heart and your soul!

The Body

Anatomy –Actions- Appetites

The body is the LEAST of who we are.

On my list years ago, I just had one major thing under the category of BODY. I wanted someone taller than me! I figured if I had to look up to a man, I didn't want to look down in the process. That was my little pet peeve. In school, I was always taller than most of the boys and girls, so as an adult, I didn't want to relive my slumping years. I didn't say what color skin, what size physique, or what color eyes. I just wasn't that given to how they looked if I could get the rest of my list filled. Of course, there are basic physical things that are important, but I wasn't particular. Having had so many diverse friends as a kid, I've learned to see and look for the good in people outside the outward appearance.

I think the same way today. We all want someone we are not scared to wake up to, but other than that… my list was done! We can be so concerned about the anatomy that we may miss something much more important. I would never say ignore that part of you and what you want. Just know, in light of the other qualities, the body is the one thing that will definitely change over the years. Changes can occur every day - health challenges, stress, the addition of children, tastes that adjust over the years, or convictions of one or the other to change something for the better.

Another thing that you should consider about the body is appetites. These can be anything from what your partner loves to eat, whether they are health conscious, junk food junkies, meat eaters or vegetarians.

I recall a couple I worked with years ago in premarital counseling. He was an avid meat eater, she was a strict vegetarian. She thought they would work through their differences as they went, but that was not the case. You have to be honest about the person you are thinking about dating and their obvious appetites. Differences may appear in the movies or music they enjoy. They can also be seen in their desires. If someone has a tendency to like casual drinking, don't think it will change. That is something that would be adjusted if needed between them and God. Some appetites are sexual. In today's world, these can run rampant. So be honest. You have to at least talk about some things so you don't go home with a purchase you didn't even read the care instructions for. Many of you may have a list in the body area that is MUCH more extensive than mine, and there is nothing wrong with that. Just be sure you understand that the body is the LEAST of who we are. Question: If you found someone who loved you beyond words and was willing to care about you, respected you in a way you could only dream about, but they didn't LOOK exactly like you want, what would you do? Try to remember what is really important beyond the smallest part of us. And don't forget, everyone has a list. Including the person looking at you.

Shopping List Conclusion

Write your list! Before you accept another date, understand what is important to you and discover what is important to them. Life is too short, and we only get one swing. Every good sports team evaluates the opponent and reviews their playbook. It is vital to know yourself and what you want. Know our non-negotiables, your desires, and what looks good on you. Learn about yourself before going "shopping." Know what you are willing to do and what price you are willing to pay to get what you want. Every relationship comes with its own price, and we can't continue expecting a lot for a little. We can't think that the other person needs to approach us with our top-five requests, but we bring nothing to them. Most of all, remember that, you, too are being shopped for! Someone is looking at you and wondering if you would fit in their world. The messages you send can turn away or attract the right or wrong person. Learn to be yourself, be honest about who you are, and allow others to do the same. If something is not a good "fit," it is OK. The world is full of other options. Open your mind to what is most important to you.

Now, take time to put some quality items on your shopping list. Once you are done… let's head to the Fitting Room!

MY SHOPPING LIST

SPIRIT

SOUL

BODY

THE FITTING ROOM

I'm not talking about physically "trying" people on. I'm not saying get in the bedroom and make sure you "fit." That is by far the LEAST concern you should have in the fitting room.

All I needed was a simple black skirt. The store set up was decent since it was early in the afternoon; not too many people around. After browsing, I finally found what I thought was going to be my perfect fit. Since I had extra time, I figured I would stop in the fitting room to ensure it was adequate. I often avoided the fitting room and would sometimes take a chance on taking my purchases home. That worked well for me in the past with some clothes, especially when I was younger and a bit thinner. But this time, I knew I needed the skirt for a special occasion and wouldn't have time to exchange it. So there I went, into the dreaded fitting room. It didn't disappoint……I mean it did, but it was an <u>expected</u> disappointment. Not only was this room musty with the smell of urine, there were clothes everywhere. I never could understand any space being left like that, especially early in the day. So of course... I left.

Fitting room experiences can often put a damper on your shopping day, but trust me, don't overlook or avoid this step. Yes, you may be able to grab some things off the rack and take them home easily, but that is with clothing. When we're talking about people, you need a moment. No...for relationships, you may need months or even a year or so in the fitting room! Now before you let your mind wander... let me explain.

I have heard about someone trying people on like they try on shoes... making sure they "fit." I'm not talking about physically "trying" people on. I'm not saying get in the bedroom and make sure you fit. That is by far the LEAST concern you should have in the fitting room. Mainly because your flesh (body) is the least part of you. Many people have found that they FIT sexually, but they forget that there is so much more to them than that. Since your body is the LEAST part of who you are, let's look at what you should be examining in the fitting rooms of life.

SPIRIT FIT

This area of your life will, without you realizing it, dictate the rest. Even if you are not deeply spiritual, it affects how you live and how you love. Not just love for each other, but how you love people in general. It will dictate how you deal with things pertaining to life. Are you spiritually compatible? Do you believe the same things about God, about people? Do you fit in how you love others? Do you have a similar or same belief system? If not, this can throw you later when you have children or when disagreements or challenges come. If you have an underlying belief that is similar, you really have a way to deal better with life's issues. Many people ignore this step because there is so much more they want. So they skip this and leave it to the end when they are already in a relationship and problems surface. That is the wrong time to realize you are not a good fit. When you know you fit here, it changes how you disagree, how you fight or don't fight. There is an underlying understanding of what is right and what is wrong. Without that, everything is a target, everything can turn into an issue. In-laws are good candidates for a disagreement, but if you truly believe everyone is valuable no matter how they act, if you believe forgiving is possible and people deserve chances, it changes how you disagree. For believers, it means how you respond to God, what you know He has said about everything, and how you trust Him in it. Do you both really strive to understand God's word and follow it? Are you both hungry and growing in your faith daily? What are the boundaries that you live by? What is negotiable, and what is not? Do you Spiritually fit? If not... let's be honest. If you decide to go forward, this should be seen as an "As Is" relationship. (See Alterations: Chapter 5)

Expecting someone to change their belief system because of you is asking too much. I once heard someone say, "Anyone persuaded against his will is of the same opinion still" meaning, they never really changed. They just did it to appease someone they cared for. Changing people is not in your control. That person and God are the ones who can initiate life changes. You can be there to help, encourage, and pray, but why spend your time trying to convert or change someone who may never want to be changed? That is what is called unequally yoked or a bad decision.

SOUL FIT

This part is fun because it deals with our likes and dislikes! It is finding if you fit in your mind, how you both think, where you want to live, how many children you want or don't want. This is the fitting room area that we spend quite a bit of time in. We like talking about what we want in life and our hopes and dreams. This area makes you laugh and makes you cry. This is where you can find a connection with music, movies, or life. If you are shopping around and the person you are connecting with does not like to talk about anything, you need to press more. This needs to be a fit that works. Many issues can come up in this area if you don't talk about what you want often since people outgrow a lot as they mature. While counseling another couple we found the woman had many allergies and her fiancé had an expectation that would compromise her health. He was not willing to change, and when we asked how she would deal with it… she simply said, " I will pray about it." We tried to tell her she was going to need more than prayer since this was not a spiritual matter but a health concern. But she kept her answer the same. She was going to pray about it. Well, that didn't work. Prayer does not change a person's will without their permission. Within the year, they were divorced… irreconcilable differences. Some things need to be considered honestly in the fitting room. Knowing what you like and don't like is important. How clean you are and what you consider too much spent on a pair of shoes may seem simplistic now, but more often some marriages are lost in the simplest ways. This is one reason we need quality time in the fitting room. Some things you won't find out in a month or two. You may need to see this person in every season of life. Winter, spring, summer, and fall! The Bible says it is the little foxes that spoil the vine. That is because a large fox may do some outward damage to the vine, knock off a few leaves, break a small branch or two, but the life of the vine is still intact. The little foxes (small disagreements) can get in and irritate your roots, the place where the life of your relationship is fed. They can often go undetected and can leave your foundation exposed to the elements, causing great damage to a seemingly otherwise strong relationship. So the more you understand the fit in your Spirit and Soul, the better the chances for a real deal!

BODY FIT

"What do you really want?"
Is there something more important to you than appearances?

Some may think that fitting in our body is just sexual, but it is so much more than that. When you deal with the body, it means the physical body and all that comes with it. The anatomy of course is just what it is, the body and how it looks. Let's talk about this for a moment.

It would be a lie to try and act like we never pay attention to how someone looks. That is the first thing we see. I have never heard anyone say, **"OOOH, Look at that woman, her spirit is gorgeous!"** or **"Girl, did you see his soul?"** No, we see the body first, and typically if we can get past that, then we are introduced to everything else. Remember when I said earlier that our body is the smallest part of us? Well it is, but so many of us have missed a real deal because that is what we judged by. Some of the most faithful and considerate people who are a great fit, are not always clothed in the perfect body. They may not be wrapped up in a bodybuilding physique, some may have a little more weight on them, others not enough. Some may have learned humility and acceptance by their own fight with self-image due to an attribute they don't really care for in themselves. If you are in the fitting room of life and all you can see is the physical attributes of someone, you have really missed a lot. Many men and women have bypassed opportunity to meet and connect with others just because of this one area. If you really want a real deal, a good fit, you may want to consider opening your mind to more than you have been open to before.

Now I realize there is nothing wrong with wanting what you want, but the question is **"What do you really want?"**

Is there something more important to you than appearances? If so, you have to adjusted your shopping list, at least to consider what you perhaps have overlooked.

The fitting room is a messy place. It often has reminders of someone else who has been there. Our past relationships can hinder us from really being honest in the fitting room. It is not the best place to be, but trust me, if you want a good fit and don't have time to be running back and forth returning things… you want to spend some time in the fitting room. Ask the same questions that you would while trying on clothing:

- How does the garment make me feel?
- Is this a good fit for my life and purpose?
- Does it bring out my better qualities?
- Does it help hide/camouflage my challenging areas?
- Is the fabric irritating or causing unnecessary discomfort?
- Can I live and feel good with this item?
- Do I genuinely love this?
- Is it too flashy or too boring for my personality?
- What is the purpose of my purchase? Does this meet it?

Take your time in the fitting room. As with clothing, the time you spend in the fitting room checking your reaction to this item will prove to be worth it in the long run. After all, your relationship should last much longer than your clothes.

THE ALTERATIONS SHOP

We have always been told not to get into relationships trying to change the other person.

We have determined that one way to identify a real deal is that it fits. If something does not fit, it is not a good deal. Some of us already have plans when we shop to alter anything that does not fit just to make the purchase. Instead of spending all of our time shopping around for something that already fits, we figure we can change it and add or take away what we don't want and make it perfect for us. We don't always consider the cost of trying to adjust it or the fact that <u>we</u> may change after the alteration. Some outfits don't have enough fabric to handle extensive alterations, neither do people. We have always been told not to get into relationships trying to change the other person. We hear it, but somehow we fool ourselves into believing that is not our motive. The biggest question you should ask yourself about these encounters is: **Am I happy with this person as is?**

Honestly, some garments require sight adjustments for the best fit. I get that. But in our relationships we should understand the difference between a simple adjustment and a complete overhaul. When we alter things, there's no guarantee we can reverse it if we change. When taking in a pair of pants, they don't normally keep the fabric in case you gain a few pounds. Once you alter it, it is done. With clothing we can just go shopping to replace it if the alterations no longer fit our life or body, but with people- that doesn't work. When we alter people, we cut away from the fabric of who they are. Anyone who wants change in their life needs to buy into it on their own, without our help. If not, some alterations can mess them up for good.

AS IS: NO REFUNDS!

When I worked in retail, we often got returned items that were opened or missing a button or belt. We would put it back on the sales rack with a special tag that said "As Is." It was understood that if you purchased that item, ONE: you could not return it. TWO: no special discount would be given for anything else you found wrong with it. It was priced and would sell at the set price "As Is."

Numerous times a shopper would purchase an "As Is" garment, then try to return it. They decided they were not willing to deal with what was already seen as "wrong" with the garment. We would call the manager and listen to all the reasons the customer decided they didn't want the item anymore. And each time, the manager would remind them, this item was purchased and tagged "As Is," no returns. What would happen to our marriages if we thought about each person coming with an "As Is" tag? No more trying to change them or return them once we get them home. No more acting as if we are disappointed that they are not what we want, when we already had an opportunity to see them as they were. If we are honest, we really need to pay more attention to the quality or how things are made before we take them home.

I learned long ago that if you expect something and don't get it, you are disappointed. But if you don't expect it and get it, you appreciate it. That is what we found with many couples. They often had great expectations that were not met, and that became the thorn of their existence. But when they didn't expect some things and someone willingly did, or gave something extra, they seemed to be more appreciative because it was unexpected.

Are you willing to have an "As Is" who does not like to clean? Maybe an "As Is" who does not like to cook? Expecting her/him to learn just because you are now together sounds like an issue in the making. Sometimes we want something that we don't want to give, or we expect people to judge our intentions but we judge their actions. We hope people will look past our attributes that are not desirable, but we expect them to meet everything on our list.

The beauty of marriage is the affliction of marriage. We are two imperfect people who God is using to perfect each other. Which means, none of us will ever have it all together. No matter how we package ourselves, no matter how we look from the outside, none of us will have it all. We will NEVER meet and marry a perfect person. There are none. The gift we have in relationships is the acceptance that we give to each other, the patience that we give, and support we lend as each of us tries to honor God and walk in our purpose. So when you see what is in front of you, realize all that editing and altering often works on clothes, but not on people. The worst thing you can tell someone is I want you, but not like this. Who you are is not good enough for me, regardless of the price. Sometimes we don't say anything. We just make plans in our mind to change what we don't like. If you have to make that many alterations to be happy, just let them go to someone who can appreciate who they are and wait for your real deal.

MEN AND ALTERATIONS

Stores often have alterations shops set up in men's departments for convenience. Most of the time a man buys a suit, it requires changes. Let's be fair to the men when it comes to alterations. Men may be programmed to think in terms of modifications without even knowing it. That is important for women to know so we don't take it personally. When they get a suit… a decent suit, it doesn't even have a hem in it. Other parts of the suit are purposely left undone to allow for changes. As women, we don't like the thought that we are made for men or that as the Bible says "her desire will be towards her husband." I'm not going into that - don't want to lose the women - but truth is truth. Men automatically think in terms of what works for them. Women, if you find a man who thinks of you first, don't despise it. Scripture talks about men loving their wives as they love themselves. If a man takes care of himself and looks to take care of you as well, it benefits both.

When a man gets a suit altered there is a better chance he'll keep it because it fits. The only thing that minimizes the altered suit is growth or changes in him. So when we talk alterations, men, remember in the back of your mind, even when you think you are not trying to change a woman, you might still be.

WHY ALTERATIONS DON'T TYPICALLY WORK

First: We are wonderfully and uniquely made. Every person is created for a purpose. Who we are is necessary to do what we are made to do. Even when we are not fully aware of exactly what we are born to do, we need to find out before we start cutting away from who we are. All of us need to refine who we are for purpose, not just for an individual person. Refining for purpose will always help because your purpose is always connected to people. Some outfits are almost impossible for a great seamstress to alter. If it's unique and has a unusual purpose, it's hard to change. The best you can do is try to adjust where it matters most.

Second: Altering for a dating relationship does not guarantee that it will make things work, because people change. What you need and want today may not be what you need and want tomorrow. Making someone change just for you is unfair, not to mention the resentment that builds when someone realizes they did all that changing and it didn't help. When it comes to people, it has to be a decision they make. We can be there as they try to find themselves and give guidance to help, but not try to change them.

Thirdly: Altering without considering the fabric of a person is a guaranteed disaster. If I add a stretchy fabric to a firm fabric then wash and wear it, I may have a ruined garment. In the same sense, some of us have attributes that JUST DON'T FIT! Instead of trying to get someone to fit, leave them alone. The fabric of who they are will never really fit, even if the color matches. It may look good initially and the stitching may looks sound; but time.. wear, and tear in your relationship will reveal the mismatch. Just let them go, and find someone made of the same fabric that you are. It will save you a large amount of drama and costs.

Alterations Summary: The bottom line is this: For an alteration to work, you have to consider the original design and quality of both fabrics. To make successful alterations, BOTH fabrics have to be considered and it only works well if they match from the beginning. The wear and tear of each fabric should be considered, and time and attention should be given to decide whether or not the alteration is really needed.

Fabric that actually fits and is put together properly wears and fades. The same is true for a life lived together. Though over time the relationship may not look like it once did, it can still be fitly joined and happy.

Expect changes in each other as you grow together. The person you connect with should not be the same person 5-10 years later. We can choose to loosen ourselves or to tighten up loose areas to fit better with someone else. Every choice is just that, a choice that should be reserved for the one who needs to adjust.

UNREALISTIC EXPECTATIONS

WOMEN: I spoke to a lady recently who has never been married. She was raised with a standard passed to her by others, as well as her own. When I heard what she expected in a husband, my first question to her was, ***"Who is that man? I'm not sure he exists!"*** If she thought he attended her church, he was probably already gone. If she thought he was on her job, he owned the business and lived out of town in a faraway place. I didn't know any man who fit that bill.

Women, if we want a better result in our dating, we need to be open, not settling for less, but planning for more than we have asked for or imagined. Sometimes our asking is off. We want so much without paying much for it, but sometimes those wants are hidden in pain or other areas of life that didn't produce well for us. If we are not careful, we can end up getting what we looked for and living unhappily because they didn't meet the real need.

First, we have to deal with our neediness. How needy are you? What are you not doing with your life because you are waiting for a man to meet everything that's lacking? Having friends and a good relationship with your family takes them off the hook of having to be everything to you at the same time.

Women know we will spend a lot on something that is completely uncomfortable if it looks good. Some of the shoes we wear - you look at them and know they must hurt! But as long as they go with an outfit, as long as they fit the look we want, the purpose we have in mind; we will not only buy them, we will hurt while we wear them. ***It is time for us to stop hurting while trying to look whole.*** Being whole in yourself means really knowing your value outside needing others to validate you. Is it is okay to consider a man who is not as financially stable as you are? One management decision at your job can change that anyway. Being open to who he is and what you both want in life outweighs who makes the most money.

If you are a man or woman with children at home, you don't have time to play games with who comes around them. Your priority should be your children but also understanding that you don't have to put your life on hold in the meantime. But you have to consider your children. You don't marry for them, because when they grow up they won't be there anyway. If you can't find someone who fits your life, purpose, and your children for now, you may need to wait. Your children are part of you and deserve you, whether you are married or not. Overall, women, if where you shop is not producing favorable results, shop somewhere else. Be open to who is out there and who may be a real deal for you.

MEN: I also spoke to a man who told me what he wanted in a wife. I had about the same reaction. When I reminded him what he was bringing to the table, he kind of blushed. Our expectations are out of control in light of who we really are. They are out of control when we examine what is necessary for us to really enjoy life and live abundantly. Instead of looking at others and what they bring to the relationship, look at who you are and what you bring.

Men basically know what they want. Men, if you are single and want a relationship, the biggest thing to realize is that you are being shopped as well! Sometimes it doesn't seem necessary to work on yourself when there are so many women out there looking. But depending on what you desire, you may want to be sure you are worth shopping for. The balance of that is realizing that even if you are a great catch, that does not mean a woman is willing to adjust her entire life to you. You have to see, appreciate, and celebrate the gift she brings to the relationship.

I have spoken often to a man who is in his mid-40s. He has never been married, and in his mind, it is the women's fault. He has an interesting background that includes a little petty crime and a few substance issues. He has a hard time holding a job and gets upset if anyone reminds him of his past, but in his mind he is a gift. And to be honest, he actually is. He has a great heart and really loves hard, but the problem is twofold.

1: He does not think that his background matters. He does not try to improve himself. He just thinks women should look past what they see or know about him and see his heart. He feels who he will ultimately become outweighs who he has been. Problem with that is not everyone has an imagination strong enough to see past who he has been and the pattern of who he is today. If he at least showed signs of personal improvement, maybe a woman would take a chance with him.

2: He is too picky! The second thing that is a hindrance to him is what he is looking for. Because he thinks so highly of himself, he is aiming real high for a spouse. He feels he can get any woman and does not want to settle for less. He is not thinking of whether or not he can actually <u>afford</u> her. He just wants her to validate his worth. Of course, you can't tell him that, but he is really shopping beyond his means. Even if he could convince a woman to marry him, either she would be dissatisfied because of the adjustments she has to make to be with him, or he would be haunted by the ones he has to make to please her. Be flexible. Know the basic "nuts and bolts" of what you really need and build from there. No one is going to be perfect- none of us are. So, men, understanding that what you want and need is key.

What you want may not be what you need, and if you are too stubborn, and picky, just like the women, you may be alone for quite a while.

Overcoming Traditional Expectations

If you are willing to look beyond your own prejudices and boundaries, you would be surprised at the good deals around you. What works for one person may not work for another. Imagine this - a man who works well with his children and a woman who works well outside the house. We would tell you that is not a good fit because it is not traditional. Or a young couple that enjoys traveling and their work does not allow them to see each other every night, but they are faithful and committed to each other and to their God. For some, that might not work. But someone may see the benefit of finding someone who is open to that arrangement. That is why we need to know ourselves, know our purpose, and know our God. He can give you unusual insight into what will help you fulfill your purpose and who works for you despite the thoughts and opinions of others.

TWO KINDS OF KNOCK OFFS

<u>The Original Knock Off:</u> A knock off is defined as: a *'copy or imitation of someone or something popular, an item intended to look like something it is not.*

It may look exactly like an original product but lacks the expensive designer label and is replaced with a fake one. Usually costs half the price with half the style appeal.'

Since I am not a huge shoppers, it still amazes me the price people are willing to pay for an item with a brand name. No problem if you like it, it just astonishes me. But in the same sense, if I were going to pay the price for a brand name, I really want what I am paying for.

The worst thing in relationships is getting and having to pay for something less than what was presented to you. No one is trying to be something less than desirable, so pretending to be something better than we are, can be tempting.

I remember a movie that highlighted a woman who was preparing for a date and ordered food from a nice restaurant and pretended that she cooked it especially for him. She threw flour around the kitchen and made it look like she really worked hard. I have seen this played out in many movies, the man who pretends he made reservations or wrote a poem he took from someone else. In the viewers mind, we share an understanding that EVENTALLY he or she is going to find out you can't cook or write poems!

When we talk about knockoffs, we basically understand what we are talking about and we don't like being fooled. It is one thing to find that someone looks a little different without make up or when their clothing is removed, it is another thing to find that the core of a person is completely different than what they presented to you during the dating time.

When someone adjusts and changes things just for the 'sale', that is an ORIGINAL Knock Off. If what you present to people while dating is not what you intend to be, or are capable of being in a marriage, you are a Knock Off. Sometimes we pretend we like sports, certain movies, or pretend that we are financially secure or responsible. To know you are not what you present is deceptive, and eventually, with a little time and observation, you will be exposed!

The Unintentional Knock Off: just as we understand the Original Knock off, we have to be honest. Not everyone that looks deceiving is trying to. Take the man who dresses down all day long, and drives a truck, but unbeknownst to us, he owns a large home, ample savings and has all his bills paid up. The well-dressed woman that is educated with high goals that she is on track to fulfilling. She could really be a simple country girl that loves to cook but also loves to dress. Not everyone is what they appear and since we often judge people by their appearance, we may end up believing they are a knock off, when it was us that made the call without getting to know them. If we take a little more time, we may find that most people are actually who they are, we just have to look closer.

HOW TO AVOID BEING FOOLED

One of the best ways to determine what you are getting… is time. People can fool you a lot of the time, but not all of the time. We are capable of operating outside of who we are for a little while, but we will always revert back to who we really are. Time is the thing that checks the label on our life. In the same sense, people who may look one way to us, time lets us see more of them than what we see at first. Thinking that someone is showing you ALL OF THEM in one setting is unwise. No one can be really known in a moment. You can believe in LOVE at first sight, but you will never LEARN at first sight. If you want to avoid being fooled either by someone else or by your own prejudices, trust what you hear from people who love you and pay attention to those closest to them, their associations can tell a lot. How they consider or treat their family is also a tell-tale. Don't ignore it when a man disrespects his mother or a woman speaks harsh about her father, especially if the mood changes because of it. No matter how much they may appear to be authentic, there are issues that may need further study. It may not tell all, but you can find out more if you take time and look close enough.

To assist in understanding different shopping styles, we put together a Shopping Survey. The varied results were interesting and helpful as we compiled this book. This next chapter will describe the results.

SHOPPER'S GUIDE FOR WOMEN
Survey Results

Women are known to shop! Stores are set up primarily for the woman shopper since she is basically the one who shops for the children, herself, and often her man. Our survey supported that theory as well. Of course, I had a greater response to the survey from women than men. Not too surprising, after all we were talking about shopping. In this chapter, we will go over the results from women.

Here is a summary of what we found in the women's survey:

The majority of women surveyed shop all the time! Whether online, in stores, or by catalog. The result ranged from all the time, to every day, to twice a month, and more. Some more conservative older women shop every few months. The younger they were, the more they shopped. Women surveyed shopped for clothing, shoes, jewelry, and simply… deals. They look for comfort and style first, second comfort and quality, and last versatility or camouflage. Women surveyed shop primarily at malls, then multi-item stores, and on occasion specialty shops. They were split on the thrift store shopping. Many said they shopped thrift and second hand because of style, cost and items that are not duplicated easily. Others have not gone thrift shopping because they are not keen on wearing what others have worn. (For dating, that can speak to people previously married.)

Of the women we surveyed who liked shopping online, they said it was due to convenience and the ability to compare prices without having to travel. Those opposed to shopping online cited uncertainty of the item purchased, the quality of fabric, the feel of it, or correct sizing.

Some women didn't care if something was a brand name. They want quality along with something they like at a decent price. Those who prefer brand names said they chose them because of an assurance of fit and quality, not just the name. Most women said they will often purchase simply because they like the item. Some consider what is popular and trendy, though most didn't, as long as they liked the item. (which speaks to men needing to be likeable not just rich or cute) Women have so many different shopping styles. Where they go, why they go, can't really be summed up in a few words. They change based on what is available. Women can make something work that didn't work last year and can go from one level of shopping to another with a single outfit or occasion. (which means women really need a shopping list or we are subject to forget what is important when we meet someone who fits the moment)

If you are not driven by comfort in your clothing, you need to realize that relationships are more important than clothes! You don't want to be in a relationship where you are not comfortable, and you don't want to be paying a high price for something that lacks quality.

Women, take time to understand your shopping habits so you can get a good idea of your dating habits. Some habits are good to keep, others may be hindering you. Knowing the difference will help you adjust so you can be found or find a great life deal.

SHOPPERS GUIDE FOR MEN
Survey Results

We assume that men don't like shopping, but that assumption is not really true. It may be they don't like shopping with women or shopping like women shop! But there are many men who love to shop. In fact, some are ALWAYS shopping.

Men are interesting creatures. They know what they want. They basically want it all - quality, comfort, style, and affordability. Men are avid window shoppers. They are always shopping, just not always buying. We found three basic categories of male shoppers. Understand that within these three groups, you will have an adventurous (high) end and a conservative (low) end in each. (This does not describe the character of a man as high or low, just the shopping pattern.)

Three Types of Male Shoppers

1 Mr. White Socks: Some may describe this man as – Clueless. This man may shop simply to meet his needs. He does not shop often, but he has "his store" that he frequents to get whatever he needs. He has no desire to try other places because this store works for him. He may window shop but doesn't typically buy unless he is in HIS store. It will take a lot to get him to venture out of this area, because he is content. He may have various colors of the same shirt or pants because they fit, are comfortable, and work. When it comes to style, he has his own. He is aware of what is available but may be uninterested in shopping and acquiring trendy items for himself. Even if he pays attention to what is out there, (since men are avid window shoppers), he is still not buying it. He is an easygoing guy who wants to be comfortable and wants his purchases to be affordable. Everything else is extra and unnecessary. (Remember there is a slightly adventurous side of this man as well.)

2 Mr. Nylon Socks: We can describe this man as having a clue, but he can't always put it together. This man knows what he likes and dislikes. He will shop beyond one store, but does not have the time or know how to put clothes together. When he is in a relationship, the woman may buy much of his clothing. If she is stylish, he is, too. People may say, "Did your woman buy that?" And he may answer, "Yes, she gets all my clothes." He is not ashamed of this. He rather enjoys the gift she brings that betters him. Beware, he is still very opinionated about what he wants and does not want, but appreciates and benefits from the help. This man can graduate easily, with mentoring, to the next group.

3 Mr. Multicolored Socks: This man could have designed the clue and can give it to you! This man loves to shop. He knows the trends, sets the trends, and can help you if you let him. His tastes can be as vast as his imagination. He may have many custom suits and shirts in his closet. But he can also find gold in a thrift store, in a shopping center, outlet mall, or high-priced department store. He looks for style and quality. He is not moved too much about price. He is willing to pay it sometimes even if he can't afford it. But if he is wise and really can't afford it, he knows how to find the next best look. This man is more likely to look for brand names. He has expensive taste and doesn't waste time on things that are made cheaply. This group is a combination between men who ONLY want brand names and the ones who can make anything work.

Men and Comfort

Most men are not trying to be uncomfortable just to look good, (unlike women with our shoes). When they shop, comfort is in the back of their mind. A shirt collar that is too tight, shoes that hurt, or pants that don't fit right do not work for most men. They are not typically trying to just look good at **any** cost. So if he connects with a woman and it gets uncomfortable, meaning there is too much drama to deal with her, they tend to think in terms of refunds. There are some men who will try to avoid the inconvenience and drama of refunds by keeping their purchase while looking for something/someone to replace it.

Men and Refunds

If a man realizes something does not work for him, he WILL refund. If something does not deliver what he wants, if he can't do anything with it or it does not do what it is supposed to do, he will refund. It might take him a while to decide to end a relationship, and unfortunately he may window shop at the same time he is thinking. This often causes a lot of confusion as if the window shopping made him make the decision, but it was probably more than that. The White Socks man does not like anything about shopping. Since it takes him so long to decide and to venture into the shopping arena, he is the most likely to keep his purchases. For dating, he might be the man who stays in a relationship even though he is not happy. (Women, don't take advantage of this man if you get one. Make him happy, and he may be the most loyal of all.)

Men and Online Shopping

Men shop online primarily for electronics and gadgets. They like to surf for the best price. Our surveys dealt with personal items like clothing, so for men, that might be ties or accessories. For something they actually want to buy, they prefer stores or shopping in person. Not strange that this comes from the need to verify fit and feel of items they buy.

Men and Personal Alterations

We talked earlier about men and how they automatically think in terms of alterations when they shop. Men themselves don't want to be altered. If you get them and accept them "as is," they are happy. Does that mean that they are perfect and always wonderful? No, but truthfully they don't want someone trying to make them someone they are not sure they want to be, though some women often try. Men, since you realize you don't want to be made to change, you have to do the alterations yourself based on your purpose, what you want in life, and what you offer to those around you. If you are looking for someone to just take care of you, many of those women are not there anymore. Learning to care for yourself and being able to share tasks at home from cooking to laundry is attractive. Women are pickier than ever and want a man who takes care of himself and cares about how he looks and still considers her. Being open to ideas from others can help you, much like the tailor who lets you know why your shoulders need to be taken in, or the waist needs to be loosened. Be open even to what other women have said about you, not the heavy criticism, but the constructive criticism. If everyone is saying the same thing, there is a good chance they are not all wrong. Again, if we want quality, we need to be quality. Just remember, as you are shopping, someone else is shopping for you. We are all basically… On the Market!

ON THE MARKET

So far we have talked about the shopping experience from the perspective of shoppers. Let's flip the page and see the perspective as the item being shopped for!

When I worked in retail years ago, one of my strengths was displays and organization. I didn't like racks of clothes in disarray, folded sweaters that were out of place, or incorrect sized groupings. I took special care to keep my department shop-able. Meaning, the customer didn't have to go through everything to find what they wanted. The merchandise was where it was supposed to be, and the mannequins displayed new arrivals combined with coordinating accessories to encourage purchases. That gift of displaying and merchandising left me over the years. I found myself in a rut and couldn't get out of it. Life does that to us sometimes, and we don't even know it. Whether it is a lack of funds, time, or drive that robs us of our desire to look good everywhere we go, we need to go back to the time we took more care of how we look and how we act. I remember when it was a big deal to go the airport and fly somewhere. Everyone got dressed up just because they were traveling. Now people wear actual pajamas on the plane. Times have really changed. If you are on the market (single and wanting to be married) and you want someone to find you, they need to see you. Not just at your best, but at least not always at your worst. **We use the excuse that people need to accept us as we are, and if they don't like what they see, oh well. But do you hold yourself to that same standard?** Now is the time to examine ourselves and be honest about what we show others. Many of you have this area down when it comes to makeup and clothes, but that deals with the body! THE LEAST PART OF US. How do we look in other areas? What do we show people about us every day that might not be the truth or might be a horrible truth? In a time of social media, you are always being shopped. Every post you make, every photo you share, every video you like says something about you. We may not think our little rant toward someone of the opposite sex affects our dating, but be sure it will. People can "shop" you without your knowledge (secret shoppers). Companies do it with their employees or potential employees. Don't think people who have an interest in you are not paying attention to your social accounts and overall appeal. In light of that and our everyday encounters, here are some things we need to be aware of while on the market.

BE GENUINE

The most important trait when you're on the market is to be genuine. No one wants a knock off. One of the greatest suspicions of brand names is whether or not we get what we pay for. Whether someone is paying a great price or an inflated price - if we choose to pay it, we at least want what we believe we are getting. You can't be genuine if you don't know yourself and the One who made you. This is not the time to attempt to be impressive. Know yourself, your good qualities as well as the challenging ones. Be honest and have a process to work on real issues. You can't be anymore genuine than YOU, but know God is always working on us to make us better on purpose.

REFINING

Alterations are what someone changes in you. Refining is what you allow God to change in you. One way that we fight being genuine is by trying to accommodate what someone else wants. Dating is not the time to change who you are specifically for one person. It is a time to allow someone else to see you for who you are, not who they simply hope you will be. The decisions to refine yourself should be based on your purpose and where you are going in life, not who you might meet. No sense trying to change for someone who may or may not be there for the journey. If you understand how who you are fits with your purpose, then you know what parts of you cannot afford to be altered. Always strive to become the best you that you can be.

HOW DO I LOOK?

Another area we fight being genuine is in our appearance. Today it is so easy to look one way one day and a completely different another day. Especially for women. We can add hair, color, nails, lashes, puffy lips, dramatic eye brows, padding in clothing - all kinds of things we can do to please someone. If you choose to adjust and enhance your looks, be sure it is based on what you honestly like, who you genuinely are, not just what is popular and trending. It is the same for men. Know who you are and how your purpose connects to how you present yourself. If your jeans are always torn and dirty, you are saying something about yourself that may not be true. Even if you are not skilled in shopping or cleaning your clothing, that is no excuse. There are too many services that can assist you. If you had a stylish father, there is a good chance you will pick up on his style. If men around you only wore jeans and sweats, you may tend to do the same unless something different draws your interest. Take time. Adjust toward what connects you to your purpose, which is the most genuine you can be.

Another aspect of how we look involves how we speak and present ourselves. If you have a lot of negative things to say about men or women, people believe what you say when they have nothing else to go on. Again, be genuine but understand you may have some rough edges that need to be smoothed if you have serious issues with the opposite sex. Being whole in your emotions allows you to honestly connect with someone else. No one wants to take the brunt of your previous bad relationships. Overall, if we want to attract quality people, we should be quality people.

ADDING BENEFIT

Since you are on the market, you should know how you add benefit to someone else. You are automatically designed to add benefit to others. There is something in you that does it without much effort, something that simply needs to be refined and tapped into. There is nothing more attractive than someone who is comfortable in their own skin and are doing something they love. The joy they get in seeing others benefit from their contribution of talent or skill shows on their face. The most attractive people in the world are working their purpose! Don't get caught up in wondering what someone else is bringing to the table in a relationship when you're bringing nothing. Your whole life, even outside dating, should involve the value of you. What benefit do you bring to the world simply because you are here? Every day is an opportunity to do more, be more, and see more benefit of being yourself.

BE WHERE YOU CAN BE FOUND

You can draw people easier when you are in the right place. If I need for something for my car, I won't look for it in the toddler department. Nor would I look for bread near the fabric softener. Where you hang out says something about what you are looking for. If you are not a messy person, don't hang around mess. Your associations speak about you. If you are a purposeful person, be found in your purpose. Be around people who are working their purpose. If you are a Christian, attending church, volunteering, and being active speaks volumes. Let your surroundings advertise for you! Understand if you are not very social, you will need to make a point to extend yourself beyond your house - places you work, worship, shop, or events you may attend. You may also find that online opportunities or referrals from friends are viable options.

BE AFFORDABLE

We were bought with a price and are basically…priceless. So how can we put a price on ourselves? We can't, but we can be affordable. Don't go into relationships expecting people to do and be everything you need. They can't. If you always need someone to do things for you, pay things for you, buy things for you, make you feel loved, valued and whole…that is defined as HIGH MAINTENANCE. If you don't have peace on your own, a relationship will not bring it to you. If you don't have control of your own finances, a relationship will not guarantee that either. In fact, it might get worse. If we want to be affordable, that lends to being whole on our own. A life out of control is costing you and anyone who is connected to you. That means mastering your life as best you can with God's help before you look for someone to unite with. The blessing of a relationship should be a dual blessing. What you bring should benefit your partner just as what they bring benefits you, but that should never be the goal. The goal and greatest value should be the person, not what they bring.

SHOPAHOLICS AND DATEAHOLICS

This chapter we will deal with dating issues that can cripple your attempts to have a meaningful relationship in the future.

I have watched television shows with my children featuring people who live in homes overcome by trash, clutter, and debris. Even in the midst of the mess, they spend so much money for things they don't need, will never use, and often don't even know where it is in their house. We have often watched and wondered why they have not spent a little of their funds on a maid! It is easy to look and criticize someone's life without understanding the underlying reasons. Some shows offer us a better look into the pain involved for those known simply as hoarders. The pain from personal losses or dysfunction can be a real issue that causes them to live in a way I am sure they didn't dream or plan for.

THE SHOPAHOLIC

So far we have talked about quite a few shopping habits. This chapter will deal with one that can cripple your attempts to have a meaningful relationship. Though it seems like "shopaholic" is a term made up by people who help us keep our credit in order, this is a real issue. So if shopping and dating can be considered similar, it stands to reason a shopaholic and dateaholic can, too. When I considered adding this chapter, my prayer was to reach someone dealing with this in their relationships so they could find clarity and freedom. If you genuinely have a problem you can't control, there is nothing wrong with getting help. Talk to a professional if your issue is severe, or at least confide in someone who can offer you an ear and accountability as you live out life. It may take much more depending on who you are and what life has already dealt you. If you fall in any of these categories, realize your life, purpose, and future love will typically have to deal with the residual effects of what you do today. The next page contains info about Shopaholics and Dateaholics.

SHOPAHOLICS AND DATEAHOLICS
How it looks and what to do…

SHOPAHOLIC Symptoms	DATEAHOLIC How it looks	START SOLUTION
EMOTIONAL SHOPPING This is seen in emotional shopping due to depression, changes on the job, trouble at home, or the need for validation. Sometimes shopping just to feel better about what you can't change.	**EMOTIONAL DATING** You may be a bit needy and insecure. Things going on in your life may cause you to go on dates you really don't want just to feel better or valued.	You're wasting time, energy, risking emotional health and not really solving any real issues. This can lead to emotional debt. Step back and find you, build your image without anyone else. Work out the life issues and begin again.
THE PERFECT ITEM Searching for the perfect item can lead to over shopping while you are looking for it. You can find things that ALMOST work, but it can cause depression for having spent too much… again without getting what you wanted.	**THE PERFECT ONE** Looking for the perfect mate. Can cause you to run through a lot of them, often "paying" more than you planned. After a while you realize you have spent much of yourself and still don't have what you started looking for.	Figure out what you want, what you need. Understand that no one is perfect, they are not coming in your life to make you happy. Stop "paying" for relationships that you don't want while looking for the one you do.
EXCESSIVE BARGAIN SHOPPING Excessive bargain shopping has you running around looking and buying deals even when you have no need. You can end up buying stuff you don't need just because it is on sale.	**EXCESSIVE DATING** Dating for no reason, but you feel you at least can afford to. You may have no desire to keep the relationship, but you are creating extra baggage and cluttering up your world so you can't even find what you need when you need it.	Sometimes we feel we can date often just because we have time and someone is available. Don't waste time with someone who is easy to come by. They are also easy to go and clutter your life. You don't look attractive to someone who thinks you already have what you want or need.
SHOPPING AND RETURNING No solid thoughts into what you want BEFORE buying. Results in many returns that in turn creates more shopping trips. You may feel justified in the process because the money used was already spent.	**IN AND OUT OF DATING** In dating, if you don't know what you want beforehand, you are subject to getting in and out of relationships. We justify excessive dating because it is not the person we really want, and we keep looking and leaving people that don't work but we still desire to connect.	Write your shopping list. Be honest with what you actually want and need. You have time! Stop rushing into relationships. You will find it does not work. Plan what works and what does not for you. Take your time and be willing to say "No." You have that option.
OBSESSIVE COLLECTING Obsessive collectors don't feel complete until they get one of each item.	**OBSESSIVE DATING** In dating this may look like trying every kind of man or woman you can.	Who we are is more important that what we have done, if we want to live better, we have to do better. **Remember this behavior not only hurts you, but also others.**

LAYAWAY!

Have you ever felt like you were alone in a relationship? Maybe that somehow the person you loved forgot about you?

I love layaway! I recall many purchases that I have used this service. I purchased furniture, clothing and many other items on layaway. I recall when I first found out about it, I just thought I could leave stuff there as long as I wanted, until I got the full amount to get it out. But, it wasn't long before I realized it didn't work that way. I had to first give an investment, then I had a set amount of time that I was allowed to keep the item, and had to make timely payments to show that I was interested in paying it off. The items stayed in layaway until the final payment was made.

FINAL THOUGHTS

The biggest lesson this book offers is the understanding that we are creatures of habit. We know something is a habit when we do it without thinking. We often feel when we shop it is well thought out, other times maybe not so much. But if we think and select the same way, that becomes a habit. I have a type of milk and a brand of milk that I always buy. If it is not there, I wait. That is a habit, not that there is no other milk in the store. If you continue to get what you have gotten from relationships, the problem might not be the people, it might be the habit. If we change our habits, we can change our relationships and make them better.

Relationships are meant to be a blessing. They are made for us to love and be loved, for us to grow and be challenged. When we are outside relationships, we are outside God's will. Don't get me wrong. I am not talking about just marriage. I am referring to all of our relationships, including parents, children, friends, siblings, extended family, in-laws, and more. Relationships are here to help us. When we think it is just about us, we've missed the point. If we think we can function and thrive in life without the connection to others, we are wrong. Some things we desire to do and be will never happen without the input or influence of others.

I love and thank God for all the people in my life; the good ones and the challenging ones, (You know who you are!) because they have helped me grow and become. Not everyone is tolerable every day, but I have learned compassion from those who are very different from me. If I had the decision to make, I am not sure I would have chosen some of the people throughout my life. Because of my own mindset and comfort level, I would have eliminated some and probably missed out on great benefits from each one. Some of the most difficult people, have taught me the most precious lessons. In every walk of life, we find opportunity to learn.

The final thought I would like to leave you with is that you are a Spirit being. No connection with another person will ever take the place of the connection with your Creator. He, Himself knows you like no other ever will. He knows how you will change over the years, because you <u>will</u> change over the years. He is the one who can help you make day-to-day decisions that can benefit you, your purpose, and the great number of people who look to you. You can't afford to miss out on knowing Him. I can't write a relationship book and forget about Jesus Christ. Because of Him, I have peace in my mind and in my home. I have a way out of every situation that seems unfixable. I have learned how to work through the additions and subtractions of relationships in my life. I can understand and appreciate the gift of people and all that comes with them. If you don't already know Him, I pray you will trust Him with you. Rely on His wisdom in your life and know that He loves you more than any man or woman ever can. I pray everyone reading this will know that God will be there to help you make good decisions as you seek Him. My prayer for you today is that you find LOVE. The true love that comes from God alone. And as you continue to connect with Him, you will see the many opportunities and blessings in others. My prayer is that you will connect with people that mean you good, who will undergird you and support you in your purpose as you support them. My prayer is that you will lead a wonderful life that includes whoever you and God allow in. I pray that you will enjoy and appreciate the people all around you, that wisdom follows you every day of your life, and you will always know the love and guidance of the Holy Spirit as you walk in your purpose. I pray that when you leave this earth, you will have made an indelible mark on humanity, for the Glory of God, and people will have enjoyed and benefited from the gift of you. That is my prayer!   ~Jacqui~

ABOUT THE AUTHOR

Jacqui Hill Goudeau is an author, speaker, and blogger with a 40-year professional journey that spans a wide spectrum from retail, radio announcing, talk shows, to prison, children, and adult ministry. Friends consider her the ultimate storyteller. Her writings include *Embarrassing Faith*, *Goudeau Gumbo for the Soul-* (a collection of poetry), and *Departed Friends, Good Grief,* (which addresses the issues of loss.) *The Single Wife*, *If You Ever Wondered About Me*, and numerous children's books. Jacqui writes from her soul, making her books all-inclusive and easy reads for men and women, Christian and non-Christian alike.

Jacqui has a witty sense of humor, which people love. In her spare time, she loves gardening, painting, and watching movies with her family. You can contact her at www.wisdomspeakstoday.com for speaking info or other books.

www.ingramcontent.com/pod-product-compliance
Lightning Source LLC
Chambersburg PA
CBHW070205100426
42743CB00013B/3058